LIVING TREASURE

Laurence Pringle

LIVING TREASURE

SAVING EARTH'S THREATENED BIODIVERSITY

Illustrated by Irene Brady

MORROW JUNIOR BOOKS · NEW YORK

The author thanks Dr. Eric Fajer, Museum of Comparative Zoology, Harvard University, for reading the manuscript of this book and helping to improve its accuracy.

This book is printed on 100 percent recycled paper.

Text copyright © 1991 by Laurence Pringle
Illustrations copyright © 1991 by Irene Brady
All rights reserved. No part of this book may be reproduced or
utilized in any form or by any means, electronic or mechanical,
including photocopying, recording or by any information storage
and retrieval system, without permission in writing from the
Publisher. Inquiries should be addressed to William Morrow and
Company, Inc., 105 Madison Avenue, New York, N.Y. 10016.
Printed in the United States of America.
1 2 3 4 5 6 7 8 9 10
Library of Congress Cataloging-in-Publication Data
Pringle, Laurence P.
Living treasure : saving earth's threatened biodiversity /
Laurence Pringle ; illustrated by Irene Brady.
p.   cm.
Includes bibliographical references and index.
Summary: Discusses the rich variety of life on earth, the origins
of such diversity, its rapid loss, and how to save organisms from
extinction.
ISBN 0-688-07709-9. — ISBN 0-688-07710-2 (lib. bdg.)
1. Biological diversity conservation—Juvenile literature.
[1. Biological diversity conservation.   2. Extinction (Biology)]
I. Brady, Irene, ill.   II. Title.
QH75.P753   1991
333.95′16—dc20   90-21463   CIP   AC

With love for Heidi, a living treasure
—L.P.

CONTENTS

"How strange and wonderful is our home, our earth, with its swirling vaporous atmosphere, its flowing and frozen solids, its trembling plants, its creeping, crawling, climbing creatures, the croaking things with wings that hang on rocks and soar through fog, the furry grass, the scaly seas. To see our world as a space traveler might see it, for the first time, through Venusian or Martian antennae, how utterly rich and wild it would seem. . . ."

Edward Abbey

INTRODUCTION

As the twentieth century draws to a close, many scientists believe that humankind faces three great threats. The first threat is nuclear war. The second is worldwide climate change—global warming.

The third threat to human welfare is less well known but no less important. It is the rapid loss of the earth's rich biodiversity, its variety of life—the only living things known to exist in the universe. Unless this massive loss of life is halted soon, some scientists believe that humanity faces a catastrophe even greater than nuclear war.

Many people support efforts to save elephants, pandas, whooping cranes, and other popular species. Meanwhile, however, other organisms are perishing by the thousands, without notice. The mass extinction now under way has been a quiet crisis because many people do not understand the value of what is being lost for all time.

This book explains why little-known and even unknown kinds of animals and plants are living treasures. It explores the rich variety of life on earth and traces how such a great diversity has arisen. Finally, *Living Treasure* describes the causes of this terrible loss of life and the steps people must take to save our planet's unique organisms before it is too late.

1

HOW MANY PASSENGERS ON OUR PLANET?

Pick up a handful of soil anywhere on earth. In it you will find more organisms—visible and microscopic—than exist on the entire surfaces of other planets.

The planet Mars is icy cold—and lifeless. The planet Venus is fiery hot—and lifeless. Between these planets lies our home, Earth. Its atmosphere makes it an oasis in space, with a favorable climate, abundant water, and a rich variety of living things.

Scientists are dazzled and puzzled by the diversity of life on earth. No one knows how many different kinds of plants, animals, and other organisms there are. But we do know that the organisms identified so far are only a small fraction of all living things. There are millions—perhaps many millions—that await discovery.

Beyond the cold, lifeless moon lies the earth, home to a wealth of living things.

The study of living things is called biology (*bio* is a Greek term for "life"). Scientists who study living things are called biologists. And biologists have a name for the earth's incredible variety of life: biodiversity.

The first step toward understanding this biodiversity is naming and describing the different living organisms. Throughout human history and all over the world, people have given names to animals and plants they recognize. For example, in New Guinea, hunters can name sixteen different frogs, seventeen lizards and snakes, more than a hundred birds, and many more insects and worms. The New Guinea hunters are walking encyclopedias of information about the life around them.

Besides naming things, people have tried to make sense of the earth's biodiversity by considering similar organisms to be members of groups. The modern system of naming and classifying living things was devised by Swedish botanist Carl von Linné (Carolus Linnaeus) in the eighteenth century. At that time, Linné and other scientists believed that perhaps 50,000 kinds of organisms lived on earth.

Since then, more than 1.5 million kinds, or species, have been discovered and named. They include 250,000 species of flowering plants and 41,000 kinds of vertebrate animals. These animals with backbones include about 4,000 mammals, 19,000 fishes, about 9,000 birds, and more than 10,000 reptiles and amphibians. The largest group by far is the insects, with more than 751,000 named so far. The remainder includes worms, spiders, fungi, algae, and microorganisms.

Biologists believe that most of the earth's flowering plants and vertebrate animals have been discovered. They estimate that only a few thousand more fishes, birds, reptiles, and other vertebrates are likely to be found. The greatest riches of biodiversity remain to be discovered in the world of insects and other small creatures without backbones (invertebrates).

Biologists expect to find some of the earth's undescribed organisms liv-

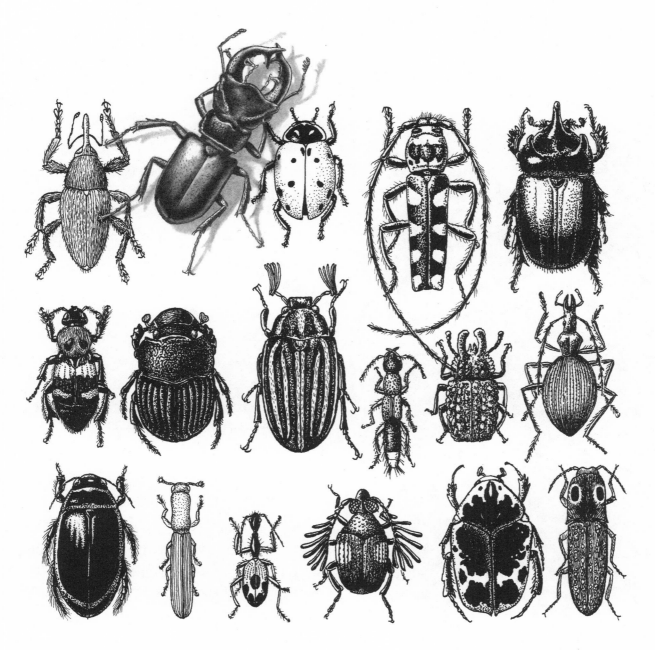

Beetles are an incredibly diverse group. A million or more species of these insects may exist.

ing in coral reefs. There also may be other undiscovered habitats, and species, on the floor of the deep ocean. In the 1980s, using small research submarines, scientists began to discover new forms of life—crabs, fishes, shrimps, tube worms—near geysers of hot, mineral-laden water that spew from the ocean floor.

The earth's greatest riches, however, lie in tropical rain forests. In the 1980s, as funds for tropical research increased, biologists found astonishing numbers of animals there.

In Panama, entomologist Terry Erwin of the Smithsonian Institution collected insects from nineteen trees of the same species. On those trees alone, he found more than 12,000 different kinds of beetles. He estimated that one out of seven species lived on that kind of tree and no other.

Erwin also collected insects from one tree in the Amazon rain forest of Peru. He sent the ant specimens to be identified by biologist Edward O. Wilson of Harvard University. Wilson found forty-three kinds of ants, including several new spe-

Deep in the ocean, scientists are finding animal species that have never been seen before.

cies. This diversity of ants—from a single tropical tree—equaled the number of ant species that are known to live in all of Canada or Great Britain.

Tropical forests are also rich with plant life. In Borneo, a botanist discovered 700 species of trees growing on ten separate plots of land that totaled about twenty-five acres. This matches the number of tree species growing in all of North America. Also, the trunks and branches of rain forest trees are habitats for mosses, ferns, lichens, orchids, and other plants that grow far above the soil. In Costa Rica alone, more than 1,100 species of orchids have been identified.

In the 1980s, Terry Erwin and other biologists began for the first time to study insects, plants, and other organisms that live near the tops of tropical trees. The organisms living in the treetops, or canopy, of a rain forest are different from those living on or close to the ground. More than half of all rain forest species may live aloft. Most of them never touch the ground. Terry Erwin has called the tropical forest canopy "the heart" of the earth's biodiversity.

Until the 1980s, biologists estimated that 3 to 5 million species live on earth. However, since large numbers of tropical insects and other organisms may live on just one kind of tree, or in one small area of tropical forest, the biodiversity of earth may be much greater. Terry Erwin has estimated that the earth may be home to 30 million species of insects alone.

The total of all kinds of life could be much higher. Rain forest canopies harbor not only insects but also unknown numbers of mites, roundworms, fungi, and other small organisms. Little is known about life in tropical soils. And most animals have other living things, called parasites, living on or inside them.

Whether the total number of species is 5 million, 30 million, or more, we know very little about the biodiversity of our planet. Our ignorance is great.

Suppose the number of species is "only" 10 million. This means that we

have perhaps discovered just 15 percent of the total number of species. Then consider that we have not yet learned much about the plants and animals that *have* been identified. Many of these organisms are "known" only in the sense that a few individuals are kept as preserved specimens in scientific collections and that they have been given a formal name.

Their lives are a mystery. Their links with other living things, their importance in nature, and their possible value to humans are also mysteries.

Many animals and plants live high in the rain forest canopy and never come to the forest floor.

2

PUZZLES OF DIVERSITY

Why are there millions of kinds of living things on earth? Why aren't there just a thousand? Why aren't there a billion?

The answers to these questions can be found by understanding how species develop. First, it is important to define what a species is. It is a population or many populations of an organism that have many characteristics in common. One of the most important characteristics is that individuals of a species interbreed with their own kind but not with members of other species.

This definition works well for most animals and some groups of plants. There are exceptions though. Mallard ducks, for example, have a distinctive look and other characteristics that distinguish them from other ducks. Under some circumstances, however, they reproduce successfully with other kinds of ducks. (The offspring, called hybrids, have characteristics of both kinds of ducks.) By a strict definition of the term, mallards and the

A mouse that escapes from a coyote may reproduce and thus pass its characteristics on to a new generation of mice.

ducks with which they interbreed are not true, separate species. This illustrates that nature doesn't always fit definitions or categories devised by humans.

Ever since life began on earth, perhaps 4 billion years ago, new species have developed through a process called evolution. It occurs because of variations in the genes of individual organisms. Genes are molecules or groups of molecules that are in the cells of each animal and plant. Even such simple organisms as bacteria have a thousand genes. Most mammals, including humans, have about 100,000 genes in their cells. Flowering plants have 400,000 or more. Genes are like a set of directions that determine the characteristics of the offspring when plants and animals reproduce.

All of the genes in all of the individuals of a species are like a bank, or pool, of information. (In fact, biologists often refer to the "gene pool" of a population or species.)

Whenever animals or plants produce a new generation, the parents' genes are combined in new ways. You have probably heard people say, "She

Genetic "directions" from both parents produce a child
with a combination of their characteristics.

has her mother's eyes" or "She has her father's chin." Each person inherits characteristics from both of his or her parents. The result is a new and unique individual.

This combining of genes can also lead to changes in the characteristics—and the gene pool—of whole populations or species. Such changes usually occur after many generations and perhaps thousands of years. Sometimes the changes lead to the evolution of a new species.

Plant breeders and animal breeders can produce new varieties of organisms; for example, different breeds of dogs. This is accomplished by selecting individuals that have different characteristics and crossbreeding them. In nature, a process biologists call natural selection also leads to changes in the characteristics of offspring and eventually to new species.

In any new generation of plants or animals, some individuals have characteristics that improve their chances of living long enough to reproduce. For example, a mouse that has an ability to avoid being eaten by a fox or coyote will be likely to live long enough to reproduce and pass this ability on to the rest of the gene pool of the mouse population. Mice lacking this ability are likely to be killed before they reproduce. Through this natural selection process, over many generations the whole mouse population may become better able to avoid certain predators. Of course, natural selection may also lead to the evolution of foxes and coyotes that have improved ability to catch mice.

If the earth had just one kind of environment, all living things would be adapted to that environment and there wouldn't be much variety. But our planet has many, many environments. Each environment has special conditions, and each one provides opportunities for the process of natural selection to bring about the evolution of new species.

The earth's geography has played a major role in the evolution of its life. First, some individuals of a species become separated from the rest of their

Erosion of the Grand Canyon separated populations of the tassel-eared squirrel. Those isolated north of the canyon, called Kaibab squirrels (left), now look different from other tassel ears.

KAIBAB PLATEAU

NORTH RIM

GRAND CANYON

GRAND CANYON VILLAGE

population by a mountain range, body of water, or other barrier. These individuals form a new population in a new environment. As the separated populations reproduce, generation after generation, they usually begin to differ from one another. Eventually, as a result of natural selection, the two populations differ so much that they would not interbreed even if they one day come into contact. They have become different species.

Oceanic islands provide many examples of this process of speciation. Storms sometimes blow birds or insects far from their homeland, out to sea. Most perish, but some reach a distant island. They are geographically isolated from others of their kind. In their new environment and over many generations, they evolve into species quite different from their ancestors.

Several examples exist on the Galápagos Islands in the Pacific Ocean about six hundred miles west of Ecuador. The islands are 3 to 5 million years old and have never been geographically connected to the mainland. Until people began to visit with ships, only a few kinds of plants and animals, carried on the wind or riding on floating objects, reached the islands.

One organism that reached one of the islands was a species of small finch. It eventually evolved into thirteen distinct species on different islands. The different species of finches vary in size and also in feeding behavior. Some eat seeds on the ground. Others feed on cacti. Still other species catch insects in trees. But they resemble one another in many ways—evidence that they evolved from a common ancestor.

Animals and plants that reached other oceanic islands also evolved into new species. This is especially true of the Hawaiian Islands, which are the most isolated on earth, and of Madagascar, which has been separated from eastern Africa for more than 100 million years. These islands are homes for thousands of organisms found nowhere else on earth.

It is easy to imagine the isolation of an island in the ocean. However, living things on continents can also be cut off from others of their kind. In

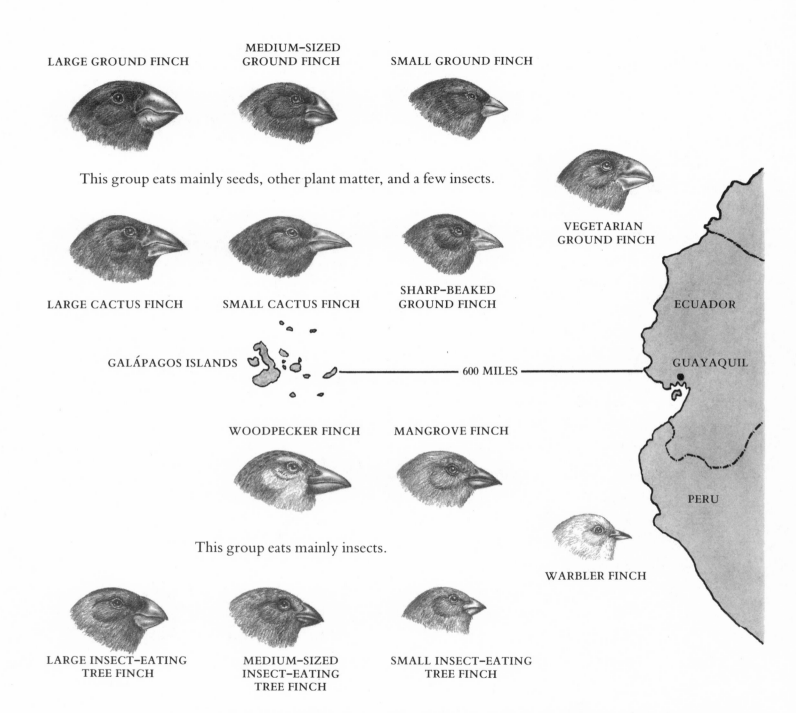

LARGE GROUND FINCH

MEDIUM-SIZED
GROUND FINCH

SMALL GROUND FINCH

This group eats mainly seeds, other plant matter, and a few insects.

VEGETARIAN
GROUND FINCH

LARGE CACTUS FINCH

SMALL CACTUS FINCH

SHARP-BEAKED
GROUND FINCH

ECUADOR

GALÁPAGOS ISLANDS

600 MILES

GUAYAQUIL

WOODPECKER FINCH

MANGROVE FINCH

PERU

This group eats mainly insects.

WARBLER FINCH

LARGE INSECT-EATING
TREE FINCH

MEDIUM-SIZED
INSECT-EATING
TREE FINCH

SMALL INSECT-EATING
TREE FINCH

After reaching the isolated Galápagos Islands from South America, a species of seed-eating ground finch grad-
ually evolved into thirteen distinct species.

24

1986, botanist Hugh Iltis of the University of Wisconsin Herbarium wrote of a "wonderland" of rare plants he found in the Andes mountain region of Peru. He collected specimens from dry Andean valleys that were like islands on land. Each valley was separated from other such valleys by cold mountain tundra above and wet tropical forests below. These barriers of climate have created separate worlds in which many plant species have evolved.

From an airplane, South America's Amazon rain forest looks like a uniform carpet of green. But a closer look reveals that it, too, is a patchwork of habitats providing places where new species can evolve. Rivers in the Amazon Basin may have played a role in creating many different habitats. Through millions of years, the rivers have changed course countless times. They shift about, leaving abandoned channels called oxbow lakes that eventually become forested land. Often that land is cut through again by a meandering river. In this everchanging landscape, parts of populations are isolated and there are opportunities for new species to arise.

Within a patch of rain forest or any other habitat on earth, there are also natural forces at work that may spur the evolution of new species. One such force is competition. Each kind of habitat—forest, desert, coral reef—provides a certain amount of space, food, shelter, and other resources needed by living things. Biologists have found that animals and plants aren't usually locked in direct competition for these limited resources. Instead, through the process of natural selection, organisms evolve in ways that allow them to share the resources.

Biologists have studied different species of reptiles, birds, rodents, and other animals that at first appeared to compete for food or other resources. Research showed, however, that each species mostly used resources that were not used by others. In a desert, for instance, two species of seed-eating rodents coexisted by choosing different-sized seeds to eat.

Other examples of resource sharing were discovered by Terry Erwin

when he studied hundreds of beetle species living on a single kind of tropical tree. He found that some beetles fed on the trees, some on fungi, some on fellow beetles, and some on dead plant and animal material. The beetles also "divided" resources by living on different parts of the trees and by being active at different times of the year. Different species had evolved in ways that avoided direct competition for food and other needs.

In addition to competition, other forces in nature may stimulate evolution of diverse species. Biologist Kenneth Watt of the University of California at Davis studied fishes in the shallow waters around the Hawaiian Islands. At least 650 species of fishes inhabit those waters. They are concentrated at coral reefs and rocky bottoms, where there are plenty of hiding places. The hideouts are needed because predators are abundant. Eighteen species of moray eels and twenty-five of jacks live in Hawaiian waters. All of them eat fish, and they prey mostly on whatever species are most abundant at any one time. Powerful waves, tides, and storms also affect life on the coral reefs. They carry bits of food to the fish but also sweep some fish away to their death.

Kenneth Watt believes that calm waters and few predators would allow the coral reef community to be dominated by fewer kinds of fishes. Instead, the threat of eels and jacks and the power of waves and storms promote change and diversity as fish evolve in different ways that help them survive.

Coral reefs of the tropics have great biodiversity; in fact, they are called "rain forests of the sea." In contrast, Arctic and Antarctic waters harbor comparatively few species. One of the great puzzles of biology is why the variety of earth's life is distributed as it is: scarce at the poles, incredibly rich in the tropics. On all continents, diversity increases as you travel nearer to the

A rich variety of sea life has evolved in the waters around the Hawaiian Islands.

equator. There are more species of plants and animals on a given plot of land in Texas than on one in Minnesota. The same size plot in Panama or Colombia has several times the species that both states do combined.

One factor that may account for these differences is the effect of climate on reproduction. In the colder climates of Europe and North America, for example, many insects require a year in order to complete their life cycle from egg to adult. Tropical insects often complete this cycle in a month. Frequent reproduction of new generations increases the mixing of genes within populations. It speeds the process of evolution, and of speciation.

In 1989, biologist George Stevens suggested another explanation for the distribution of diversity on earth. His theory is based on the adaptation of species to the climate of their natural habitat. In temperate and polar climates, plants and animals must tolerate changing seasons, including cold winters. This adaptation then enables them to exist in a climate that varies and to live in a wide geographic area.

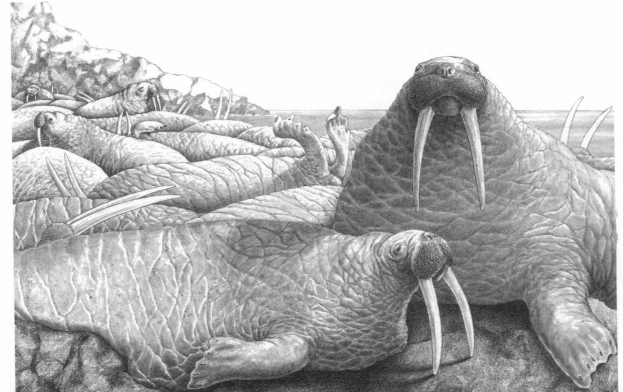

In the earth's polar regions, large populations of walruses, penguins, and a few other species may exist, but the overall variety of life is low.

In contrast, plants and animals living in the tropics experience a climate that doesn't vary much. Adapted to these conditions, tropical species are also restricted by them. Just a slight change in land elevation may produce enough difference in climate to act as a barrier for some organisms.

The 150-foot distance from the sun-drenched tree canopy to the shaded forest floor also represents a great change in climate. An organism that strays a short distance from its natural habitat may find conditions unbearable. According to George Stevens, many tropical species are adapted to very specific, localized habitats. He believes that this accounts for the rich variety of life in the tropics.

As far as biologists can tell, the diversity of life on earth has increased through time. Clues about life in the past come from fossils, although biologists acknowledge that this evidence

The short distance between the floor and the treetops of a forest may represent a great difference in climate.

is incomplete. There is, for example, a better record of hard-shelled invertebrates that lived in shallow seas than of vertebrates that lived on land. Allowing for gaps in the fossil record, however, scientists conclude that the earth's biodiversity has grown. Modern oceans, for example, contain at least twice as many species as the seas of 300 million years ago.

Biologists have wondered whether there is a limit to the earth's diversity. If the different kinds of living things number in the many millions now, could they someday total a billion species? Most biologists believe not.

Stephen Jay Gould of Harvard University has pointed out that some of our planet's biodiversity is a result of the breakup of the vast landmass called Pangaea. As parts of Pangaea separated and became today's continents, the earth's total area of shallow seas increased. (Shallow seas surround continents, so there is more of this habitat around several continents than around one huge one.) Shallow waters also became isolated from one another. This allowed many new species of mollusks, crustaceans, and other creatures to evolve.

The earth's continents continue to shift position slowly. Volcanoes erupt and mountain ranges rise, bringing change that fosters the rise of new species. However, nothing comparable to the breakup of Pangaea is likely to occur and create new, isolated habitats where numerous new species could arise.

Furthermore, biologists believe there is a limit to the number of species that can coexist in a tropical forest or any other habitat. Only so much living space, food, and other resources are available. So there is probably an unknown limit to the biodiversity of the earth.

Questions about the origin, distribution, and potential numbers of species will continue to intrigue biologists. These puzzles seem insignificant, however, compared to the question of how to prevent massive and swift loss of the earth's rich variety of life.

180 MILLION YEARS AGO

90 MILLION YEARS AGO

PRESENT

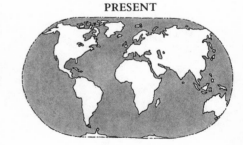

The breakup of Pangaea and separation of continents created environments where new species could evolve.

3

MASS EXTINCTION AND NATURE'S UNDISCOVERED RICHES

Like an individual, a species has a beginning, a history, and an end. When a species dies out, it is said to be extinct. Although some kinds of plants and animals become extinct each century, the earth's history has been marked by several extinctions in which untold thousands of organisms expired. The greatest mass extinction occurred about 250 million years ago, when perhaps three-quarters of all sea animals and many land animals and plants perished.

Judging from the record left by fossils, millions of years must pass before the diversity of life recovers after a mass extinction. New species evolve from the survivors, but evolution of a rich biodiversity takes a long time. The last great extinction occurred about 65 million years ago. About that

The extinction of the dinosaurs made it possible for other groups, especially mammals, to flourish.

time, all dinosaurs perished—except perhaps some small species that may have evolved into what we call birds. Many other forms of animal and plant life also disappeared.

Some scientists claim that mass extinctions can occur when a giant meteorite crashes into the earth. Others believe that the cause may be a period of intense volcanic eruptions. In either case, the result would be changes in temperature, rainfall, and overall climate that would wipe out organisms all over the earth. The causes of previous mass extinctions are still being investigated and debated by scientists.

Now the earth's rich diversity of life is again threatened—not by an object from outer space or by upheavals from within the earth, but by the actions of the human species, *Homo sapiens*.

The destruction of the earth's biodiversity now under way is like no other in our planet's history. Previous large-scale extinctions probably occurred over a span of hundreds of years. The mass extinction caused by people may wipe out millions of species in a century or less, a mere wink of time in earth's history.

Now numbering 5 billion, the human population continues to grow. It may reach 8 billion by the year 2130. People strive for food and other necessities of life. In poor nations, they fell trees for fuel or to clear a patch of land on which to grow crops. They build new roads that slice through forests. They dam rivers that flood wild valleys.

Wildlife habitats are threatened everywhere on earth, including the Arctic and Antarctic. However, the greatest blows to biodiversity fall on the tropical rain forests. They cover only about 7 percent of our planet's land surface but are home to more than half of all species on earth. As much as 80 percent of the earth's biodiversity can be found in about a dozen tropical countries. The most species-rich nations are Brazil, Colombia, Mexico, Zaire, Madagascar, and Indonesia.

The loss of tropical habitats is already great. About 25 to 40 percent of the land that once supported tropical rain forests has been cleared. During the 1980s, an estimated 27,000 square miles was lost each year. Each year's loss is an area a bit larger than the size of Costa Rica; it is also slightly larger than the state of West Virginia. The island nation of Madagascar, home of many animals and plants found nowhere else on earth, has lost 93 percent of its forests.

The area in gray shows the extent of Madagascar's eastern rain forest in 1950. The area in black shows what remained in 1985. Also shown are some of the island's native species that are now extinct.

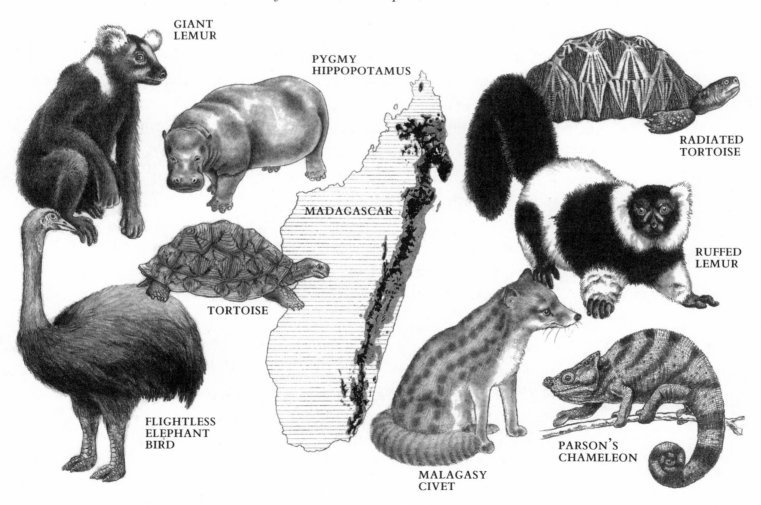

GIANT LEMUR

PYGMY HIPPOPOTAMUS

RADIATED TORTOISE

MADAGASCAR

RUFFED LEMUR

TORTOISE

FLIGHTLESS ELEPHANT BIRD

MALAGASY CIVET

PARSON'S CHAMELEON

Destruction of any tropical habitat may destroy unique species because so many invertebrates and plants exist in small isolated areas of the tropics. We can safely assume that many thousands of species have already perished in this century and that the rate of extinction is growing. In most cases, the organisms that have been and are being snuffed out are unknown. They're gone, and so is our chance to learn about them and learn from them.

Felling a forest, polluting a river—these are acts that clearly threaten the earth's biodiversity. Species also die for less obvious reasons. One is invasion by "alien" organisms. These are not species from outer space but animals and plants that people deliberately or accidentally bring to an island, continent, or other area where they are not native.

In some ways, moving organisms from one locale to another has added to the variety of life on continents. In North America, for example, such non-native organisms as the German cockroach, gypsy moth, starling, and kudzu vine are well established. African honeybees (sometimes called killer bees) entered the United States from Mexico in 1990. And, given enough time, populations of such alien organisms may evolve into new species that differ from their ancestors abroad.

Overall, however, alien plants and animals diminish the earth's biodiversity. The plants are often aggressive invaders that take up so much space and sunlight that they cause the decline or disappearance of native plants. Many introduced animals are also pests. Some have wiped out numerous native organisms.

In Africa, for example, an alien fish has caused the extinction of native species that exist nowhere else. Three lakes in Africa—Victoria, Tanganyika, and Malawi—are among the oldest freshwater lakes on earth. These lakes have been geographically isolated for many millions of years. Their fishes have evolved into great diversity—about 1,100 unique species. (In contrast, fewer than 160 species are native to the Great Lakes of North America.)

In 1960, people who wanted to improve commercial fishing released the Nile perch into Lake Victoria. The perch has since displaced many native fishes. At least thirty-five species are extinct, gobbled up by Nile perch.

Alien organisms have also caused the extinction of many species native to oceanic islands. These species often exist in small populations in special habitats and are highly vulnerable to extinction. The Hawaiian Islands once had more than 1,700 native plants that grew nowhere else on earth. Now most land below 1,650 feet in elevation is covered by thousands of alien plants. As a result, more than 200 native species are extinct and 800 are in danger of dying out.

Before people reached the Hawaiian Islands they had just two native mammals, a bat and a seal. Now they have at least eighteen alien mammals. This is a questionable gain, since such mammals as wild pigs, which feed in part on native plants, have helped cause the plants' extinction. The mongoose has helped wipe out unique species of ground-nesting birds. Because

The nene goose and other ground-nesting birds of the Hawaiian Islands are easy prey for the mongoose.

these birds had evolved their nesting behavior in an environment that was free of such a nest-raiding predator, they were vulnerable once this animal had been introduced.

Within the next century, biologists estimate, extinction caused directly or indirectly by people may destroy nearly half of the earth's plants, animals, and microorganisms. If this occurs, the mass extinction will be more devastating than the great death of the dinosaurs and other forms of life 65 million years ago.

According to fossil evidence, the conditions that caused mass extinctions in the past did little harm to plants growing on land. These terrestrial plants were a vital resource for the surviving animals, from which new species arose. The mass extinction now under way threatens the survival of many kinds of tropical trees and other land plants upon which countless animals depend for food and shelter. If they perish, humans will have caused the worst mass extinction in the earth's history.

Considering the short time in which this extinction may occur, British scientist Norman Myers wrote in 1986 that the results may be "the greatest single setback to life's abundance and diversity since the first flickerings of life almost 4 billion years ago."

Nevertheless, some people question the seriousness of the problem. They feel that extinction is, after all, a natural process. An estimated 90 percent of all organisms that ever lived on earth have died out. Besides, many of the threatened organisms are insects and other invertebrates. Are all of those beetles, ants, and mites really needed? Does it matter if the process of extinction is speeded up and the earth's one-millionth species of beetle is never identified and named?

Biologists admit that some organisms probably have no great significance in their plant-animal communities and no economic value to people. However, part of the tragedy of the mass extinction now under way is that we know so little about what is being lost. The one-millionth species of beetle *might* be a "keystone" species—one that plays a key role in the workings of the habitat where it lives. We don't know.

It was only a few decades ago that botanists learned of the vital role played by fungi called mycorrhizae that grow on or in many plant roots. They reach beyond roots into soils and absorb nutrients that are returned to the plant. If key mycorrhizae are missing, many trees and other plants cannot survive and seedlings cannot grow into mature plants.

Also, the great value of bats in tropical forests has only recently been recognized. Without certain species to pollinate their flowers, fruit trees do not produce food and highly valued timber trees cannot reproduce. Fruit-eating bats also disperse tree seeds and help revitalize forests.

No doubt there are other organisms that play vital roles that we have not yet discovered. Harvard University biologist Edward O. Wilson has urged that we assume that "all of the details matter in the end, in some unknown but vital way."

Certain organisms matter because of their aesthetic value. The sight of a butter-

Bats play a key role in tropical forests. Some pollinate flowers; others scatter seeds over the forest floor.

fly, the sound of an owl, even the scare a low-flying bat may give us—all enrich our lives. People crave nature's diversity. They visit zoos, aquariums, botanical gardens, and natural history museums to satisfy this craving.

Some people believe that all living things—every kind of spider and moss, as well as every kind of whale and monkey—are valuable simply because they exist. They are all part of the great mystery of life. Biologist George Woodwell of Woods Hole Research Center said, "One might dream that on the only green planet we know, life would have a special value of its own."

Nevertheless, biologists are often asked to justify their concern about loss of the earth's biodiversity. Do these living things have any practical use for people?

Some do, and we don't know enough about the rest to say they will not contribute to human well-being. The genes of each species are storehouses of information, and this genetic information is the earth's most valuable resource. If the earth is home to 10 million species, wrote biologist Thomas Lovejoy of the Smithsonian Institution, "they then represent 10 million successful sets of solutions to a series of biological problems, any one of which could be immensely valuable to us."

Scores of "worthless" organisms have proved invaluable to humans. One example is *Penicillium* mold, which has the ability to ward off competitive fungi. Discovery of this characteristic led to the development of antibiotics that fight bacterial infections and have saved human lives. Numerous wild plants contain chemicals that have shown some ability to combat cancer. In 1958, a chemist extracted two compounds from a Madagascar periwinkle plant that proved to be effective against two forms of cancer, leukemia and Hodgkin's disease. In 1985, the worldwide sales of these two plant extracts totaled $100 million.

More than a hundred chemical substances extracted from plants are used in drugs that doctors prescribe to control disease and lessen pain. Plant extracts are part of modern medicine practiced in Western nations and the traditional medicine used in developing countries. But only about 5,000 of an estimated total of 250,000 plants have been investigated to find out if they have medicinal qualities.

Useful medicines have also been derived from insects, worms, fishes, and other animals. From sponges that live in the Pacific, scientists have derived substances that show promise as medicines against cancer, parasites, and infectious diseases. Researchers are studying tiny tropical frogs whose poisons are used on the tips of blowgun darts by South American Indians. They believe that chemicals in the poisons could be used to help people, for instance, by controlling pain and relieving muscle spasms.

The potential of the earth's food plants is as great and as untapped as its sources of medicines. People obtain 85 percent of their food directly or indirectly from just twenty kinds of plants. About two-thirds of our food comes from three plants: corn (maize), wheat, and rice. We began to cultivate these plants thousands of years ago, mostly because they were easy to grow. But people have used about 7,000 plant species for food, while another 70,000 edible plants exist. Many of these foods offer better nutrition than the kinds we use.

Several food plants used in the tropics are being studied with a goal of more widespread use. They include the winged bean of New Guinea, a quick-growing, highly nutritious plant, all parts of which are edible. Another is the Buriti palm of the Amazon rain forest. Its fruits are rich in vitamins C and A. Yet another, the Babussa palm of the Amazon, is called the "vegetable cow." It is a rich source of vegetable oil and food for livestock.

Tropical forests are rich sources of food and medicine plants, only a few of which are now made use of by people.

39

Botanists hunt for the wild relatives of cultivated plants because these species are often found to have characteristics missing from the crop plants. Crossbreeding can produce plants with improved crop yields, better nutrition, and greater resistance to pests and diseases. Most of our foods originated in the tropics, so botanists look there for related species that can improve crops.

During a 1962 plant-collecting trip in Peru, botanist Hugh Iltis discovered two new species of tomato, bringing the total known species to nine. This was genetic treasure. After more than a decade of crossbreeding one of these wild species with cultivated varieties, plant breeders developed tomatoes with greater sugar content that were highly valued by tomato growers. In 1986, Hugh Iltis asked, "Who could have predicted that these tiny, slimy seeds of a useless, ugly plant . . . might enrich the U.S. economy by tens of millions of dollars?"

In addition to new foods and medicines, the earth's biodiversity harbors other undiscovered treasures including potential sources of fibers, fats, and oils. Also, anyone who hopes to develop new insecticides, fungicides, or herbicides can find chemical clues in tropical plants. Moist tropical habitats are ideal growing places for fungi, and, in general, the tropics are lush with plants *and* rich in insects that eat plants. So there has been an "evolutionary arms race" in the tropics. Many green plants have evolved chemical defenses against fungi and leaf-eating insects.

Clearly, the earth's biodiversity offers us *possibilities*. We cannot even imagine all of the usefulness and intangible values of its well-stocked genetic library, yet we continue to toss out thousands of unread volumes.

Some plants have chemicals within their leaf tissues that repel leaf-eating insects. By studying these plants, scientists may find new ways to protect food plants from insects.

4

THE CHALLENGE OF SAVING THE EARTH'S LIVING TREASURE

"The species extinction crisis is a threat to civilization second only to the threat of thermonuclear war. While a majority of the species threatened with extinction are still completely unknown, the results of their loss could be an unprecedented human tragedy."

This is part of a statement signed by nine prominent U.S. biologists at a national conference on biodiversity held in 1986. There was a sense of urgency at the conference, during which biologists discussed how to avoid rapid loss of the earth's biodiversity. Since 1986, some countries have acted to slow the pace of extinction, and public concern has grown.

There is no doubt that people care deeply about some animals and plants; for example, the bald eagle, which is a national symbol of the United States.

Public concern about wildlife usually focuses on appealing species, and sometimes on just a few individuals. In 1988, two gray whales trapped in ice off Alaska were rescued—at great cost.

Many people strongly support programs to save animals that they find appealing. In 1988, the plight of two gray whales trapped in ice off Alaska drew worldwide attention. A million and a half dollars were spent to free the whales—two individuals of a thriving population of 20,000.

Some observers wished that the money could have been available for improving the lot of species close to extinction. The gray whale incident illustrated a dilemma facing those who strive to save the earth's biodiversity. At times, people will go to great lengths to save certain organisms, but they don't yet care about many others.

In some cases, uninformed people actually favor the wiping out of species. Merlin Tuttle is science director of Bat Conservation International, an organization that aims to help one of the least popular groups of animals on earth. In 1988, he said, "I could proba-

Growing numbers of people recognize the value of insect-eating bats and take steps to protect and increase their populations.

bly raise ten times as much money if I promised people I'd *get rid of* all the bats in their area, instead of asking them to help me save them."

Teaching people the value of bats and many other unpopular, unappealing, or overlooked organisms is one challenge facing biologists and environmental groups. Biologist Paul Ehrlich of Stanford University said in 1986, "Many of the less cuddly, less spectacular organisms that *Homo sapiens* is wiping out are more important to the human future than are most of the publicized endangered species."

Some people are beginning to care about millipedes as well as monkeys. Also, there is a growing public understanding that habitat destruction is the greatest cause of extinction. Fortunately, when concern is focused on a few endangered species—the lemurs of Madagascar, for example—the result can be saving the habitat of hundreds of unique organisms that make up the plant-animal community of which lemurs are but a part.

There are efforts to save California condors, black-footed ferrets, and other specific species, but increasingly the goal of biologists and environmental groups is to save habitats. Setting aside preserves, such as national parks, is a vital step toward saving the earth's biodiversity. Biologists now recognize, however, that such refuges are sometimes inadequate. In some developing nations, the establishment of a nature reserve forces people from their land. Often local people do not benefit from the park. Illegal burning, tree felling, and hunting of rare animals in the park may continue.

Pollution from faraway places can also harm nature preserves. Fish, frogs, and other aquatic life in parts of Canada and the northeastern United States have been wiped out by the effects of acid rain. Much of this pollution is carried by winds from coal-burning power plants in the Midwest.

Scientists are also worried that biodiversity protected in reserves all over the world will be threatened by a warming of the earth's climate. By burning coal, oil, and other fuels, and by felling and burning vast areas of forests, people have begun to cause the climate to grow warmer. As long as this continues, global warming will affect all life on earth. There is no way to protect a national park from drought or other harm caused by worldwide change in climate. Unless global warming is stopped, species that now get some protection in refuges and parks may be threatened.

In the United States, scientists now recognize that species can be lost from very large preserves, including national parks more than 800 square miles in area. Mining and housing developments beyond park borders can have harmful effects on wildlife within. A preserve that is cut off from other wild land is like an island, and we already know that the biodiversity of islands can be easily lost.

In 1979, scientists from Brazil and the United States began a study aimed at learning how big nature preserves must be in order to halt the loss of species. Researchers worked with ranchers in northern Brazil who were clearing rain forests; they created a set of preserves of different sizes. This is the largest experiment in ecology (the study of the relationships between living things and their environment) that has ever been attempted.

At least twenty years of observation will be needed to gauge the effects of isolating the reserves—twenty-four in all—from the main forest. It is already becoming clear, however, that small plots of a few acres are worthless. The variety of birds, rodents, and insects found in them drops quickly. In one small reserve, the survival of three species of frogs depended on their being able to reproduce in the water of a wallow made by wild pigs called peccaries. The peccaries and other large mammals fled when the reserve was isolated. With no pigs to dig the wallow, it dried up and the frogs died out.

In a preserve of 250 acres, the usual variety of butterflies was able to survive only in the center of the forest. Tropical ecologists believe that rain forest reserves should be at least 125,000 acres in size in order to sustain their diversity. Some say the minimum size should be a half million acres.

In Brazil, peccaries and
other large mammals fled
when all of the forest sur-
rounding a small reserve was
cut down. Their watery
wallow dried up, and frogs
that reproduced there died
out.

47

The largest wildlife reserve on earth is in Tibet. The size of Colorado, Qian Tang is a vast territory of dry plains, lakes, and mountain ranges where few people live. Indonesia, Bolivia, and many other tropical countries have also set aside some habitat reserves. Costa Rica has a government committed to saving its rich biodiversity and the best national park system in Latin America.

In Costa Rica, extra funds for habitat preservation have been raised by swapping "debt for nature." Like many developing nations, Costa Rica has a large financial debt—more than $3 billion is owed to foreign banks. Conservation groups have helped Costa Rica reduce its debt, and in return the Costa Rican government has committed more funds to protect its habitats.

The first debt-for-nature swap, negotiated in 1987, saved a large area of rain forest in Bolivia. A U.S. group called Conservation International purchased $650,000 of Bolivia's $4 billion debt to foreign banks. In return, Bolivia agreed to protect nearly 4 million acres that surround its main refuge in the Amazon Basin, the Beni Biosphere Reserve.

Debt-for-nature agreements can help save other particularly valuable blocks of habitats. But biologists and environmental groups recognize that establishing a few nature reserves in each nation will not halt the mass extinction now under way, especially in the tropics. Conservation of diversity must somehow be made part of land use everywhere.

Because of their rich variety of life, many developing nations in the tropics are "biological millionaires." They also have great debt and growing numbers of people desperate for food, fuel, or cash. They are destroying the natural resources upon which their long-term well-being depends.

Rich nations have encouraged this folly. Millions of acres of rain forest have been cleared and burned to provide pasture for beef cattle. Most of the meat is exported to the United States and other wealthy countries where it is often used in fast-food hamburgers.

When the long-term well-being of all people on earth is taken into account, the act of destroying tropical forests in order to provide pasture for beef cattle is terrible folly.

Until the mid-1980s, aid programs for developing nations inadvertently encouraged the destruction of biodiversity. For decades, the United States Agency for International Development (U.S. AID) and the World Bank granted funds for dams, roads, and other large-scale projects without any thought to their impact on natural resources.

This has changed. In 1985, the World Bank began to review proposed developments with a goal of avoiding harm to all sorts of wild lands and waters. U.S. AID has also changed its policies.

Rich nations have always played a big role in exploiting the natural resources of poor nations. Since this will continue, rich nations have a special responsibility to influence poor nations to save their biodiversity.

With the support of rich nations, Brazil had a policy between 1965 and 1983 of encouraging forest burning, cattle ranching, and other destructive development. That began to change in 1988, when Brazil's president suspended programs that gave loans and tax breaks to projects that harm the environment. Brazil's environmental protection agency was also strengthened. The turning point came when Brazilian scientists examining satellite photographs of the Amazon rain forest counted more than 6,000 human-made fires in a single day.

Business and trade groups have also begun to show concern about rain forest destruction. In 1988, representatives of the timber industry from forty-two countries formed the International Tropical Timber Organization. They agreed that ways must be found to manage tropical forests so that timber can be harvested far into the future. The organization provided money for a study of how people in Brazil can use the resources of tropical forests without destroying them.

Some researchers have already concluded that tropical forests have more economic value to people if they are left uncut. A team of biologists headed by Charles Peters of the New York Botanical Garden reported in 1989 that harvesting fruits, rubber, oils, and cocoa from rain forests can yield twice as much income as timber cutting or cattle ranching on the same land.

Findings like this offer hope that millions of people trying to eke out a living in developing nations can be encouraged to live *with* wild habitats instead of destroying them in order to grow crops for a few years. Once natural vegetation is cleared, most tropical soils lose their fertility quickly and are abandoned. In the Amazon Basin, an estimated 40 million acres of forest have been converted to crop and pasture land, and about half of this area has been abandoned.

In other regions, there are also large tracts of cleared land that have not been reforested. They offer great opportunities and challenges. Biologists have urged that some abandoned land be planted with fast-growing trees that produce fuel wood in ten years or timber in twenty-five years. These tree plantations would offer an

Tapping rubber trees is just one way in which people can earn income from tropical forests without destroying them.

alternative to the continued destruction of native forests. About 5 million acres of such plantations have helped Burma, Indonesia, and India reduce the pressure on their natural forests.

Biologists are studying the regeneration of tropical forests. They wonder whether diverse natural forests can someday grow on abandoned land. Research shows that natural reforestation in the tropics is a slow process. Plots of an acre or two that are cleared and farmed for a few years require at least 150 years to recover completely. Much larger areas that are converted to pasture may need a thousand years.

Conservation groups and government agencies could speed this process, however, by practicing a new kind of applied science called ecological restoration. This is already being applied in North American prairies, saltwater marshes, and other habitats. By reintroducing native species and getting rid of alien species, ecologists aim to restore the diversity of natural plant-animal communities.

Applying this process to the tropics is a great challenge. So far, biologists have learned about some key factors that keep tropical forests from reoccupying abandoned land. One is that birds, bats, and rodents—rather than the wind—disperse the seeds of most rain forest trees. Yet few of these animals venture into large openings. Another factor is that most of the seeds that do reach cleared areas are quickly eaten by ants. Also, plants that do gain a roothold have a difficult time in the sunbaked, infertile soil.

Nevertheless, biologists believe that these problems can be overcome. The first major attempt is under way in Costa Rica, where University of Pennsylvania biologist Daniel Janzen has begun to restore native dry tropical forest plants to abandoned land. Large-scale programs of restoring rain forests may lie in the future.

Funds for studying the rich diversity of the tropics are increasing. We have so much to learn about life there and everywhere on earth. We know,

The regeneration of tropical forests depends on birds and on mammals, such as agoutis, that disperse tree seeds.

however, that we have already impoverished ourselves and future genera-tions by wiping out many thousands of species. As the earth's biodiversity is reduced, each remaining species with its unique genetic information becomes more precious.

The toughest questions facing humanity are not scientific. They are eco-nomic and political. Rich nations must help poor nations to save the diver-sity of life that is a treasure for all.

WHAT YOU CAN DO

The earth's greatest treasures of biodiversity live in tropical countries, but every state and province of North America also harbors unique organisms. Some are threatened with extinction; some are still unknown to biologists. People can take action to save many of them.

A vital step is protecting large blocks of habitat and, wherever possible, leaving corridors of wild lands between different reserves to keep them from becoming isolated islands surrounded by development. Every state and province has one or more agencies in charge of parks and natural resources. Many states also have programs aimed at saving rare or threatened animals and plants. Information can be obtained by writing to these agencies in your state capital.

At both the local and national level, citizens can influence political leaders to pass legislation that helps preserve biodiversity. They can, for example, write to or call their local legislator to support the establishment of parks and wildlife refuges. This lobbying of politicians is also vital at the national level.

In 1989, legislation was introduced in the U.S. Congress that would make protection of biodiversity a national goal. If the bill becomes law, it would establish a center for biological research that would prepare lists of species, populations, and biological communities that are declining or otherwise of special concern. It would also require the Environmental Protection Agency to oppose federally funded projects (such as dams or highways) that would cause extensive losses to declining species. Passage of this law will give the United States greater credibility when it seeks to influence other nations to preserve their biodiversity.

People can help save habitats, and species, from destruction by purchasing certain products and not others. For example, some environmental groups urge consumers to avoid buying products made with wood from tropical trees, since very few timber companies operating in the tropics make any effort to replace what they cut down. A list of products to avoid is available from the Rainforest Action Network (address on page 56).

On the other hand, people can help halt deforestation by buying certain products harvested from tropical forests. Environmental groups are trying to create markets for nuts, roots, fruits, oils, and other products that can be taken from rain forests without great harm to plant or animal life. In 1990, these products included a candy bar, Rainforest Crunch, made with cashew and brazil nuts from the Amazon, a hair conditioner based on brazil nut oil, as well as soaps, shampoos, and perfumes containing ingredients from rain forest plants.

Environmental groups work at the local, national, and international level to protect biodiversity. Their efforts include lobbying politicians, arranging debt-for-nature swaps in tropical countries, and buying valuable habitats outright. In 1990, for example, the Nature Conservancy bought the 321,703-acre Gray Ranch in southwestern New Mexico. The land and waters of the ranch are home to an estimated 75 species and subspecies of mammals, 150 species of birds, and 52 kinds of reptiles and amphibians.

Joining an environmental group is one way to learn about opportunities—local or global—for helping save some of the earth's unique species. The groups listed here are among the most active and effective.

The Children's Rainforest,
P.O. Box 936, Lewiston, Maine 04240

Conservation International
1015 18th Street, N.W., Suite 1000, Washington, D.C. 20036

Cultural Survival,
11 Divinity Avenue, Cambridge, Massachusetts 02138

National Audubon Society,
950 Third Avenue, New York, New York 10022

The Nature Conservancy,
1815 North Lynn Street, Arlington, Virginia 22209

Rainforest Action Network,
301 Broadway, Suite A, San Francisco, California 94133

Sierra Club,
730 Polk Street, San Francisco, California 94109

World Wildlife Fund,
1250 24th Street, N.W., Washington, D.C. 20037

GLOSSARY

biodiversity—The variety of living things on the earth.

biology—The science of living things and life processes, including the growth, evolution, and distribution of plants, animals, and other forms of life.

climate—The average long-term atmospheric conditions, including temperature, wind, and precipitation, that prevail in a particular place. A region's climate includes extremes, such as droughts, as well as its more routine weather.

ecological restoration—Efforts to restore such habitats as forests, prairies, and salt marshes to natural conditions by reintroducing native plants and animals and eliminating alien species.

ecology—The science of the relationship between living things and their environment (including other living things as well as soil, climate, and nonliving factors).

entomology—The scientific study of insects.

evolution—The process by which the characteristics of a population or entire species of organisms gradually change over a period of time.

extinction—The process by which all living individuals of a species die and the species no longer exists. Most of the living things that have existed on earth have become extinct. Past mass extinctions, involving loss of many thousands of species, were caused by climatic change or other natural events. People are causing the current mass extinction.

fossils — Skeletons, impressions, tracks, or other traces of animals or plants from past ages that have been preserved in rock. Fossil invertebrates are sometimes found in amber.

genes — Molecules or groups of molecules that are part of the sex cells and other cells of organisms and that contain chemical "directions" that determine the characteristics of the individual that develops from a fertilized egg.

genetics — The study of the heredity of living things, or how parents pass their characteristics on to their offspring.

global warming — The gradual warming of the earth's atmosphere now believed by atmospheric scientists to be under way. Human activities that add carbon dioxide, methane, and other heat-trapping gases to the atmosphere may cause enough warming to raise sea levels, change rainfall patterns, and threaten crops, water supplies, and wildlife.

habitat — The kind of plant-animal community in which an organism lives. For example, the habitat of the black-footed ferret is prairie dog colonies.

hybrid — The offspring produced by breeding plants or animals of different varieties. Such crossbreeding is done deliberately to produce livestock or food plants with more desirable characteristics, such as disease resistance.

invertebrates — Animals with no backbones, or vertebrae. They include insects, spiders, mollusks, crabs, and corals.

keystone species — Organisms upon which many other kinds of living things depend for existence.

mycorrhizae — Fungi that live on or within the roots or rhizomes of many plants and absorb nutrients from the soil that are then used by the plants.

parasite — An organism that lives on or in another organism, its host, sometimes harming it but usually not killing it. Parasites include fleas, tapeworms, and ticks.

speciation — The process by which distinct species evolve.

species — A population or many populations of an organism that have characteristics in common, which make them different from individuals of other populations. The members of a species interbreed with each other but not with members of other species.

vertebrates — Animals with backbones, or vertebrae. They include fishes, amphibians, reptiles, birds, and mammals.

FURTHER READING

Today, and no doubt for years to come, the single most valuable source on this subject is *Biodiversity*, edited by Edward O. Wilson (Washington, D.C.: National Academy Press, 1988). It presents the text of nearly sixty papers, together with extensive bibliographies, given at the 1986 National Forum on Biodiversity. Several reports from it are among the sources of information cited below.

Ehrenfeld, David. "Thirty Million Cheers for Diversity." *New Scientist*, June 12, 1986, pp. 38–43.

——— "Why Put a Value on Biodiversity?" In *Biodiversity*, pp. 212–16.

Ehrlich, Paul. "The Losses of Diversity: Causes and Consequences." In *Biodiversity*, pp. 21–27.

Erwin, Terry. "The Tropical Forest Canopy: The Heart of Biotic Diversity." In *Biodiversity*, pp. 123–29.

Farnsworth, Norman. "Screening Plants for New Medicines." In *Biodiversity*, pp. 83–97.

Gould, Stephen Jay. "Diversity Through Time." *Natural History*, October 1975, pp. 24–31.

Grant, Peter, and Nicola Grant. "The Origin of a Species." *Natural History*, September 1983, pp. 76–80.

Lewin, Roger. "Biologists Disagree Over Bold Signature of Nature." *Science*, May 5, 1989, pp. 527–28.

———"Parks: How Big Is Big Enough?" *Science*, August 10, 1984, pp. 611–12.

May, Robert. "How Many Species Are There on Earth?" *Science*, September 16, 1988, pp. 1441–49.

Norton, Bryan, ed. *The Preservation of Species*. Princeton, New Jersey: Princeton University Press, 1986.

Peters, Robert. "The Effect of Global Climatic Change on Natural Communities." In *Biodiversity*, pp. 450–61.

Plotkin, Mark. "The Outlook for New Agricultural and Industrial Products From the Tropics." In *Biodiversity*, pp. 106–16.

Pringle, Laurence. *Global Warming*. New York: Arcade Publishing, 1990.

———*Restoring Our Earth*. Hillside, New Jersey: Enslow Publishers, 1987.

Raup, David. "Diversity Crises in the Geological Past." In *Biodiversity*, pp. 51–57.

Raven, Peter. "Our Diminishing Tropical Forests." In *Biodiversity*, pp. 119–22.

Raven, Peter, et al. "The Origins of Taxonomy." *Science*, December 17, 1971, pp. 1210–13.

Reinthal, Peter. "The Living Jewels of Lake Malawi." *National Geographic*, May 1990, pp. 42–51.

Repetto, Robert. "Deforestation in the Tropics." *Scientific American*, April 1990, pp. 36–42.

Slatkin, Montgomery. "Gene Flow and the Geographic Structure of Natural Populations." *Science*, May 15, 1987, pp. 787–92.

Sun, Marjorie. "Costa Rica's Campaign for Conservation." *Science*, March 18, 1988, pp. 1366–69.

Watt, Kenneth. "Deep Questions About Shallow Seas." *Natural History*, July 1987, pp. 61–65.

Wilson, Edward O. *Biophilia: The Human Bond with Other Species.* Cambridge, Massachusetts: Harvard University Press, 1984.

Wolf, Edward. *On the Brink of Extinction: Conserving the Diversity of Life.* Worldwatch Paper Number 78. Washington, D.C.: Worldwatch Institute, 1987.

INDEX